EAST & WEST

EAST
&
WEST

poems

Piotr Florczyk

LOST HORSE PRESS
Sandpoint, Idaho

ACKNOWLEDGMENTS

Grateful acknowledgement is made to the editors of the publications in which the following poems, sometimes in earlier versions, first appeared:

basalt: "Still Life with Apples," "Night Swimming"
Charlotte: A Journal of Literature and Art: "At the County Fair"
The Laurel Review: "Pastoral," "Lullaby"
The Literary Review: "Ink"
The Louisville Review: "Tetris"
The Manhattan Review: "Last Poem for You"
New Orleans Review: "Nineteen Eighty-Nine"
Poetry Salzburg Review: "A Pole in New York," "Downriver," "Stone Age"
Slate: "Omaha Beach"
The Southern Review: "Backyard," "Rain"
West Branch: "Elsewhere"

"Ink," "Lullaby," "Omaha Beach," "Pastoral," "Stoppage Time," and "Tetris" also appeared in a chapbook of twenty poems, *Barefoot* (London: Eyewear Publishing, 2015).

This book would not exist without the encouragement and advice of my mentor Sandra Alcosser, as well as many friends, who've read and re-read these poems over the years, especially Veronica Andrew, Robin Davidson, Boris Dralyuk, Ilya Kaminsky, and Kevin Wisniewski. I am also grateful to Robert Faggen, Katie Ford, Mark Irwin, Todd Swift, and Andrew Winer for their support.

I would also like to acknowledge the support of Antioch University Los Angeles, Cecil College, Claremont McKenna College, San Diego State University, University of California-Riverside, University of Delaware, University of San Diego, and my latest home, the University of Southern California.

Special thanks to Christine Holbert and Christopher Howell of LOST HORSE PRESS for guiding these poems into the world.

Cover Art: Alison Barrows-Young, *Hoping for Rain,* Oil on canvas, 36" x 48", 29 August 2015. Other art by Alison Barrows-Young may be found online at wwwalisonbarrowsyoung.com.
Book & Cover Design: Christine Holbert.

FIRST EDITION

This and other fine LOST HORSE PRESS titles may be viewed online at www.losthorsepress.org.

LIBRARY OF CONGRESS CATALOGING-IN-PUBLICATION DATA

Names: Florczyk, Piotr, author.
Title: East & west : poems / by Piotr Florczyk.
Other titles: East and west
Description: First edition. | Sandpoint, Idaho : Lost Horse Press, [2016]
Identifiers: LCCN 2015051177 | ISBN 9780990819363 (trade paper : alk. paper)
Classification: LCC PS3606.L586 A6 2016 | DDC 811/.6--dc23
LC record available at http://lccn.loc.gov/2015051177

for Dena

TABLE OF CONTENTS

NINETEEN EIGHTY-NINE

I.

It was a strange life we lived. Strange people knocked on our doors at
    strange hours
and asked for two eggs, a frying pan. Strange how we dressed in the same
    gray suits

and hats. Remember? Our future was unpaved. If we stretched our arms
    out,
took five steps to the right or the left, there was the wall. So we moved
    little, like shadows

at the onset of night. Then you showed up, with a scoped-rifle slung across
    your back,
pushing a white, top-load Maytag on a dolly. We greeted you as if you'd
    never left.

2.

Which is why nobody noticed your breasts. The glasses. Or the stars
     tattooed on
the inside of your right wrist. The way you wrapped your hair around
     your finger,

nervous before strangers, even though you were raised on fate alone and
     then schooled
in East and West. What happened after your hot-air-balloon escape?
     Like others

from this side of sense, we got hard labor, but not as bad as grandma's
     stint at Carl
Zeiss in Nazi days. At least we knew you wouldn't grow up to toil at the
     coke plant.

3.

Everybody worked there: your father, uncle Stephen, aunt Stella, the red-
 haired twins
who lived below us. They rode together the rickety tram in the mornings,
 never

missing their stop. On weekends we fished for King carp, checked our
 place on the list
for the Fiat family car, attended Sunday mass. Then the strikes began:
 prophets

went down or up, through trap doors, over the fence. The air stung.
 Imagine the fun
we had, hunkered between potted ferns on the balcony, skipping stones at
 the enemy.

4.

Next our food rations were cut: one loaf of bread a day instead of two.
    A small
brick of butter mixed with lard per week. Hardly any meat, except chicken
    bouillon,

which we diced like a Rubik's cube. The waiting lines became the talk of
    the town.
Yesterday's news served as toilet paper. After they shut down the colleges
    and interned

the faculty, your father said that words don't grow on trees, so we read
    the way
we ate—slowly chewing each word—unsure which words we were allowed
    to keep.

5.

This is how we found out about the tanks in Budapest, Prague, Sofia,
    Bucharest.
Monks transcribing prison verse. Bards rewriting Beatles' songs for bound
    hands.

I too wanted to sing our way out of here with a guitar I got from a
    Swedish friend,
but it broke while I was being chased. Tell me, where did you learn to speak

so fluently? Ten years, and your accent hasn't changed—you still roll your Rs
and shorten those pesky Slavic vowels. (Your boots stood at attention in
    the foyer.)

6.

You told us you flew high above Europe, across *La Manche*, before the
    winds carried
your balloon back to Munich, where you were shot down accidentally.
    A refugee,

you attended a boarding school run by the Ursulines. You prayed in
    German for
those who pole-vaulted the barbed wires but would never walk again.
    Lucky for you,

you said, by the time you finished college the Cold War had entered its
    final dawn.
Still, you stayed up late, calculating how far a heart travels from home
    with each beat.

7.

If you were a boy, I would've asked how often you nicked your smooth jaw
before you learned to shave, but since you were a girl, my girl, who
    showed you

how to put a tampon in or how to fit a bra? Was there a man in your life?
    I wept,
knowing how much we'd missed. But with the neighbors coming over
    with Bulgarian

wine, your father and I kissed and hugged you instead—we didn't ask
    about the gun—
suddenly unwilling to share you with anyone, including your cousins Alex
    and Jan.

8.

Believe me, we were beside ourselves at the sight of the washing machine made
in the USA. Those buttons and knobs. The days of bending over a
   washbowl were over.

Sheathed in aluminum was a drum the size of a sauerkraut barrel, you
   explained,
and while the cycles were limited to cold and hot, the spin to fast and slow,
   meaning

there was no way for us to lose control, our faces had already been
   bleached by grins.
We couldn't wait to finally sieve, sort, and disembody the impurities in our
   garb.

9.

Or in our lives. You're free, you said to us, to do as you please. Go on —
    try it out.
But who would've thought the Maytag would work to this day. Buried
    under towels

and coats in the basement, its motor revs up dutifully, then the whole thing
    shudders,
slides like a continent towards its future. Doubtless, my daughter, it will
    last until

the final load, until the ants march it out through the back, even though
    there is
a tendency in this house to overload the guy with too much that just won't
    wash out.

OMAHA BEACH

Returning here, it hasn't been easy
for them to find their place in the black sand—
always too much sun or rain,
strangers driving umbrellas yet deeper

into their land. The young radio host said so,
speaking of the vets. When the sea had come,
some curled up inside the shells;
others flexed and clicked their knuckles

on the trigger of each wave, forgetting
to come up for breath. Then, as now, there was
no such a thing as fin-clapping fish,
quipped the host—his voice no more than

an umlaut going off the air. But he didn't
give us a name at the start or the end.
Nor did he explain how to rebury a pair of
big toes jutting out from the mud

at the water's edge. In the end, it's a fluke.
A beach ball gets lost. And a search
party leads us under the pier, into the frothy sea
impaling empty bottles on the rocks.

STOPPAGE TIME

I'm not sure how soccer
explains the world,
though books
are written about that, you know.

If the ball sneaks in, grazing
the post and the crossbar,
the upper-ninety
shot doesn't take us

into a bedroom,
where a TV's always on.
Democracy means everyone
gets to play—

regardless of who rules
the clock or the stands—
like in baseball:
our turn, their turn . . .

In another place, you
know, that fucker,
grabbing his shin and faking
a foul, would be a friend.

STONE AGE

Despite what might've happened
first, now I hear a short man,
with a square chin and eyebrows
prickly as hawthorns, calling
"monkey, monkey" after his beagle.
But the drunk isn't drunk,
at least not on the *Golden Pheasant*
I'm having. Each time
he shouts, the beagle stops,
looks back, then moves up
along the hedge colored with sparrows.
Truth be told, if the beagle
rolled its eyes, licked its chops,
or muttered something
under its breath, I wouldn't doubt it.
It's a coincidence that I'm even here,
on my parents' windowsill,
about to fly a hand-me-down
underpowered F-16. "Monkey,
monkey," the old man
waits for his boy at the boarded-up
flower shop. Deeper now, booming,
his voice rearranges the dark
inside of me.

TELEPHONE MUSEUM

Silence reigns in a hall,
where velvet pillows
and sturdy desks conjure hell
for uninitiated guests.

The tin-can telephone
sits next to a German red
rotary-dial, though most
don't ring a bell unless

they're reached by a stray
echo of 'Give me a call' or
'Don't ever call me again.
Asshole.' The window sign

hasn't been flipped in days,
but 'We're Open' really
means what it says—
even the payphone, stuck

in the corner, sans the booth
and the handle, agrees.
We've come a long way
from 'clap your hands'

or 'nod your head,' not to
mention the cordless
push-button freedom fighter,
to let someone know

their signal had carried,
but still our calls get dropped
like faded pennies. Vintage
everything, of course,

is back in vogue. Even
here, roving aimlessly while
technology goose-steps by,
we make the shaka sign

with our hands, hoping
to connect across the room
our own—what else?—
unspooled *oohs* and *aahs*.

STILL LIFE WITH APPLES

When you first bite into
a hard, green apple, and the tart
juice runs down the stubble
on your chin and neck, you

realize you know nothing
about how it ended up in the fruit bowl
you got as a gift.
So you think up an orchard

and a farmer driving a tractor.
Baskets. Ladders. Knives.
A sun that rises
and sets over pock-marked hills.

This isn't your life.
The trees change color with the apples.
You know you couldn't
look after them, but you try.

Come out, you worm,
you say to the bruised hole at the center.
Then you bite around it—and wait
for something to answer.

DOWNRIVER

The day you left with nothing
but a frayed fire-retardant blanket
and a can of pinto beans,
we thought the world came to an end.
I mean, the fridge
had sat warm for weeks,
the tap bled something black and
a garden snake
shimmied in the basement.
While I readied to pick up the dog shit
and mow the lawn,
you dined on filet mignon in Cheyenne—
or was it farther out west?

When the first star appeared,
D. and I stuck sprigs of mistletoe
behind our ears and French kissed
under the chin-up bar.
Did you see us,
atop a dune in the sandbox,
raising our arms to you?
We went there after seeing
a high school play
about a tourist who never showed
because he kept missing his train.
Left alone,
we became the rust
racing down the tongue of the slide,
the seesaw weighing the air.

Many thanks
for the parting gift of *America:
A Short Intro*—
aptly, page after page
questions get answered with questions.

See, you can't walk into the same river twice,
or so I've been told
by many who've done it at least once,
but that hasn't stopped me
from making baby sounds
with my lips
pressed against the fishbowl.

      It's time for me
to go beyond the rocks cloaked in moss
and float on my back,
like a wreath.
You must've reached the mouth
of the river long ago, though
which ocean is yours is anyone's guess.
For now, D. tells me
not to ask what's past the bend: water,
she says, always
finds a way to make you see
yourself as another.

LULLABY

Wrapped in sheets like a mummy, or a wound, you can tell it is not a
    murmur
but something lesser still that you hear when you eavesdrop on the couple

having sex next door. Their bodies, gasping and changing gears, are in
    the way—
stuck between you and some muffled yelp that travels down the dimpled
    walls.

If only they stopped ringing the doorbell, those tipsy carolers, maybe you
    could
finally hear the conch in your head. Insured by Smith & Wesson, powered
    by

Rita's Apple Pie, you won't catch any Zs tonight, since the footsteps and
    toilet flush
give way to MAYDAY being tapped on the pipe above. Is fire alarm next
    in line?

You've fed the dying goldfish, paid the gas bill . . . And now you put your
    lips on
your wife's open mouth, sorry to see it adrift on the pillow, like an island
    in high seas.

FROM THE LIFE OF POSTAGE STAMPS

The American Aspen

Unlike birches, which bring
the Nazis and frost to mind,
you got yourself a town
the rich can get behind.

But I know you flutter
in the breeze, gold though you are.
Destined to become paper,
I'd too reach for the matches.

The Fighter Ace

I tried hard, long and hard,
to get away from you,
though somehow I always managed
to do the split on the wing

and hurt myself, climbing
into my shiny Messerschmitt.
Those were the days!
I ran out of fuel after takeoff, once—

the sight of the green, green
grass forever embossed on my mind.
I learned to water-land
in dry season. They called me

'son-of-a-gun,' but I was
more than that: the Cuban Eight,
the Chandelle. On my first mission,
in '39, I pulled off

the Immelmann, only to lose
my way back to base.
There's beauty in staring
at the world, but from the air

all rivers look the same.
My own fate was sealed
when they called off the search.
Go ahead, hold me,

but you can't lick me,
unless you mean it.
You can have my Iron Cross—
rusty though it is. In turn

I ask that you don't flap your arms
at every plane that flies by.

The Weightlifter

Neither clean nor a jerk,
he stands before us,
holding the bar over his head,
more or less.

What a sexy midget —
hundred percent pure muscle.
The red singlet
hardly hides his private parts.

The six bumper plates
do what they can
to keep him straight.
He has a future in Sudan,

carrying pails of water,
should anything here go awry.
Things are getting hotter.
Hold your breath

and you'll see he's accidentally
powdered his cheeks.
What a class act —
too bad there are no Greeks

among us. The blood that flows
through his veins
can't be described in simple prose,
hence the cheers and grunts

coming from all but the judges
who keep their fingers
on the buttons while his mind
slowly lingers.

Hurry up, you white light.
Let me off the hook.
No man can make things right
while he holds the world in his arms.

The Castle

Hold your horses, everyone—
this isn't Scotland.
What ramparts have done for them,
a rusted chain-link does for us.

No wonder the drawbridge stays
down—a thirsty tongue.
After years on the job, the watchman
pisses in the moat at night,

when elsewhere the school kids
are learning how to be
the best they can be.
Ah, if the moss could talk.

Sometimes a bored clown
hitches a ride on the gun, or a pair
of ghosts hooks up inside
the royal chamber, but the legends

are buried in the dungeon.
Climbing to the top of the tower
the guests are reminded
America wasn't built in an hour.

Still they come from beyond
the tree line to see the flag, stuck
wrapped around the pole half the time,
either whole or tattered.

The Kitchenware

Between the fork, spoon, knife
and, my favorite, the two-faced
meat tenderizer, an entire
commando force can be assembled.

No one beats the wiry eggbeater
or the black spatula, even
the food processor shoved behind
the Dutch oven. A jar opener

is for sissies who've never squeezed
a tennis ball. Better they stick
to the frying pan or the wooden
citrus reamer. Tongs are fine

for dealing with sauerkraut or
Polish sausages, but they share
a drawer with the measuring cups
that often go missing.

Stir-frying noodles in a wok
is easier than it looks. The peeler
loves the grater the way
the heirloom tea cup loves the saucer.

The carafe of icy water is a beauty.
From the center of the table,
it reflects sunlight onto
the plates and mugs of mortals.

The Explorer

To con and be rad in one
breath is the goal,
although there's no poll
as to what

drives us more.
Some of us pay for the privilege
with a public visage;
others lose their lives,

friends or fortunes.
Hitting the road—the desert
or the sea—has never
been easier, and that's a fact.

Pelts, stones, routes,
peaks and continents.
Secret codes and documents.
In the name of; because;

can't stop us now.
We thrive when we're told
there's a spice we can't hold
or taste.

The natives we meet
on trips, they come in many
shapes and sizes—sound and crazy.
But sometimes we see

no one for miles.
That's when the world's flowers
and animals are truly ours.
The planets are next.

The PC

Not much can be said about it—
this depository of fading memory.
If you agree the future looks bleak,
don't click here.

PASTORAL

I was born in a city—you've never been there. I rubbed shoulders with
  buildings, blue
trams, and pigeons. Then I had this idea to take a hike and get some fresh
  air elsewhere.

The idea wasn't mine, but nor were the oaks I hugged with strangers, or
  the lashing
brook I stood in barefoot, catch-and-releasing. I followed the rules and
  stayed on the trail.

Then I changed my mind, decided to leave, but couldn't find my way back.
  The idea
was mine. I've carried it around like a breadcrumb; neighbors think I've
  got stuff

up my sleeve. So we're learning together how to cross an intersection with
  the lights
turned off, or how to tell a real turnip from a knockoff. No one complains
  if, out of

boredom, I slingshot rocks at their windows, but when I stagger with a
  story of the sun
climbing a fire escape in the rain, they ask not for the ending but for
  silence, something

like a furrow or a dagger.

RAIN

It's been raining nonstop for five days
in Los Angeles, and hardly any driver thinks
it's important to turn on the headlights.
In Europe, for example, they keep the lights on
year-round. Should we applaud?

While ruin invites rumination, light
doesn't always wait at the end of the tunnel.
For now, wading down Bundy, men in orange
smocks keep dead leaves from clogging the drains.
All other escape routes appear passable.

INK

How much did it cost me?
More than a hundred bucks
behind the multiplex—
and ulcers, gray hair.
But I had no choice: this deal
was the only one that made sense.
We shook on it.

And he handed me a box
marked *Toys for Tots* on the sides,
insisting I'd better not inspect
anything. He swore
the manual was included.
I paid him in cash
rolled up inside a fountain pen.

While he sped off
in a painter's white van,
I counted to twenty, as ordered,
and played hacky sack
with a Pepsi can.
Then I ran home, punching holes
in the walls along the way.

After I slipped unnoticed
into the house, drops of sweat
streaked down my face.
I let the printer rest
in the company of paperclips
on my Ikea desk;
it was heavier than I'd imagined.

For every button I understood,
there were many others
that baffled me, and levers

that moaned like cellos.
I got my middle finger stuck
in the paper tray,
trying to reach deep down.

At last stirred by feeling
rather than fate or fact,
I opened it up and planted a flag
of cyan, magenta, yellow, and black
in its heart.
Gently, I slid
five hundred sheets inside.

The goal was to add up again
the correspondence
I'd carried on with myself,
the maple out front,
and my wife's amber eyes—
the way they trapped my lies.
For if there was a chance

to redeem myself, this was it.
While I was shaking out
my whites at the laundromat
when we first met,
the painter said he thought of art
as windows and doors.
So I pressed PRINT

and stopped the maple
from shedding leaves.
To my wife in the next room,
bundled up like a burrito
on that cold night,
I promised not a waiting room
of dimmed lights, but a life.

BACKYARD

It's my first—and everyone I know is already here, or waiting
in line to get in. Ants, spiders, earthworms, even a pair of field mice

with BB gunshot wounds who show up at dusk. Same as newlyweds,
they bring suitcases full of sticks, tin foil scraps, dead flies, and

walnut shells packed like coffee cans with grass seeds.
If things go well, they will soon settle in the nooks of the trench,

quarry the rocks, build a shanty town in the shade of the orange cable I cut
when I tilled this hill. May's beautiful here. They will turn the young

pachysandra into tables and chairs. And why not—this place
is growing on me, too. It's near the tracks. Fenced in by tall weeds.

Half a mile from the twirling barber pole. Go on now, climb over
my calloused foot, between the muscled roots, you gypsies of the soil—

I whisper as they disappear, come knocking again. And when I peek
under the quilt of lawn, I see rooms, hands waving in the air.

TETRIS

While searching for a place to eat our sandwiches
of honey ham, Swiss cheese, we came to the edge of

a tract I once lived in, unsure why I had left,
unsure why thistles grew where a bike path had been,

and leaving you to guard the gate, I went inside
a five-story block, pretending I didn't know the way.

But the staircase remembered my stride—its wooden
planks creaked and squeaked as I climbed slowly, holding on

to the wrought-iron rail. The air was thick with flies,
the smell of fresh tar sizzling on the roof, where,

years ago, we'd go to spit on people's heads and tweak
the antennas to catch somebody else's dreams.

Life was beautiful, I thought, leaving the first floor.
I found my misspelled nickname carved into the wall.

The second story, too, held a secret I would never
forget. The teenage years. Boys chasing girls.

The painted-shut window with the view of the church.
The hollow spot under the stairs where she told me

I had to take my clothes off before she would hers.
(After she unplugged the extension cord, the light-

bulb that dangled above went out, shivering stars
around us.) Out of breath, I cleared my throat, pushed on.

Arriving on the third story, I wondered what
became of Peter and Paul. They started shaving

in junior high, grew to be six-foot-four. I'd heard
they followed the dusty footprints their father left

coming home at night, and got a job underground.
Who knows, they might well be in Dublin or Belfast,

tossing back pints in an empty pub. No wonder
the fourth floor was a blur, and the fifth why I came.

But when I rapped my white knuckles on the door,
the brownish leatherette cover caved in under

my wedding ring. So I checked the address again—
apartment 9, last building on the right, dead end

street lined with lilacs—*check*, *check*, *check*, I flipped
through memories, hoping to see the familiar eye

plug the Judas hole, hear the turning of the locks,
the clinking of the chain lifted and unhooked, dropped.

KINDERSZENEN

Nineteen Ninety-Four

From the air, patches of wilderness
      across undulating land
give way to runaway freeways and blue-
      tiled swimming pools
framed by eucalyptus. Southern California:
      gorgeous people without
grammar rich in gender and case. (On TV
      everyone claps and cheers.)
Last night I met my first tremor inside
      a Sav-On. The freckled
checkout girl didn't ask where I was from,
      or why I cut each day into
the frame of the unlocked side door,
      tracking my height, my time to go.

Looking West

These floor-to-ceiling windows
        deserve another view—something
besides the graveyard, the wispy clouds.
        The rainbow-inked
flier had dirtied my hands with promises.
        If only a single griever would
come, grasping a bunch of lilies,
        and kneel at the plaque
half-buried in the ground, the end would
        again resemble the beginning.
A trace of consolation remains
        in the distant peaks climbing
over each other like men. By sundown,
        they're nearly here.

Cape Cod

Water, water, but no fish — too bony
      to eat off a paper plate
balanced on my knees. Still, ponds upon
      ponds test my limits:
the letters I write you, having learned
      the ABCs alongside nettles,
horseflies, and the most gnarled of trees,
      sink without a trace.
With luck, I touch the bottom and catch
      a glimpse of a one-eyed
monster rumored to nestle inside footprints.
      My ship, the one I'll take home,
is a walnut shell — its figurehead
      a boy gasping for breath.

In the Heart of the Country

After winter, spring comes knocking,
        knocking on the jaws
and chests of the tools hung in the shed.
        This is not a place
to visit alone. Better go play outside,
        he says, locking the door.
Ride the water pump. The zinc
        bucket, kicked over by a pig
on the run, is a crown—try it on
        while you can. Be safe, though,
climbing the stone angel. One day
        you'll understand
the words cut in the wing by another
        trembling hand.

Europa, Europa

From behind, even the cabby's bald
        and egg-shaped head
resembled a dome. "To the city limits,"
        we said. As he reset the meter
and put the Audi in first, sweat beaded
        on the hairy stem of his neck.
The popping of bugs that stood in our way
        wasn't enough to get us
talking, until the last bored tourist
        disappeared from the mirror
and we, with time to kill, arrived in a field
        dotted by gopher mounds
and a single brass cross. "Son, you can
        never leave the past behind."

Havre de Grace

Out where the lone oak meets the beach,
    they throw their kayak
onto the bay, then slip on the orange vests.
    Like two faithful swans,
they tie up each other's loose strings —
    his trunks, her Brazilian bottoms —
and, gripping the sides for balance,
    slide into the keyholes. Suddenly
they barely escape a landing seaplane
    and tipsy anglers whose
floats disappear. "Left, right," "left, right" —
    they shout back and forth,
joining the others who've turned their oars
    into crosses and swords.

Thaw

Taught to know better, the scouts march
      through dirty snow—the shoeshine
hides the moss of their beards.
      When the chief's arm goes up,
they sign their names in piss—all winter
      they've prepared for this.
Had the creek not burst its banks, drowning
      the marker tractor tire, they
would've mastered the compass, and Steve
      would still be alive. "Coming,"
he had yelled from the lookout
      on the mace-shaped rock. While they
carry him in a poncho, the wind twists
      the trees into question marks.

In the Tropics

Like fountain statues, the surfers
      bob and spit on the waves
while we draw lines in the sand, jailing
      our own shadows.
Those who cap their bronzed ears
      with a conch, remind us
we are not alone, but the sky merely looks on.
      Here, as on the boats
that go by, with their three funnels
      spewing smoke of the deepest black,
everyone fibs just to survive.
      After three days and two nights,
the stone stairs the sea gave up
      at low tide are our only way out.

Endless Summer

As she begins cutting my hair, she
      promises I'll lose
five pounds by the end. Snip, snip—
      she takes years off
my baby face; the hairline turns out
      rounded, not squared. Watching
my blond locks tumble down the cape,
      I follow the buzzing
of the clippers, a hit of life and death,
      until the sliding door
opens and I end up on the sidewalk,
      in a pool of light. There,
staring through the glass at a pile of hair,
      I vow never to forget her.

Painting a Room

Between smoke breaks and eating
      a cheese pizza, choose
a roller that won't shed its fuzz. Then dip it
      in paint poured into a tray.
Splatter the excess onto the wall, like holy water.
      Though eggshell or mocha
blur dream and reality, the blotted
      abstraction is where you begin.
Move up and down—use force to cover
      every blemish. If this is
the kitchen—spill and splash; the next coat
      matters most. If this is the guest
bedroom, imagine the emptiness of people
      departing each year.

Homecoming

After twelve hours in the belly
       of the plane, you're speechless
in a shuttle van hurtling down the road
       past boarded-up shops
and rope-jumping kids, while your eyes—
       barely open, glazed
from alphabetizing time—twirl, then
       focus on the fonts of rain
erasing the jonquils on roadside shrines,
       until, out in the open,
someone you love throws their arms
       around your sweaty neck,
so that you can let go of splintering oars
       and wear your body like air.

AT THE COUNTY FAIR

1.

Off the Black Eye Beach, the wind puffs a whiff of tanning spray
between pickups and tents parked and pitched on hay.

2.

Those who come to crown the lamb of the Bay,
a hamlet lost in the crease of maps, have sworn not to sin all day.

3.

They trust their land was found by Spanish galleons gone astray
on the way from Manila with chests of silk and spice buffet.

4.

Fittingly, some congregate at the rifle booth of yesterday,
where every hit scores a coupon for a human-hair toupee.

5.

Hiding out on the bluff, the teens wait for the stars to array,
and their bodies follow. Police stake out the cabaret.

6.

Unlike their ancestors buried under lumps of clay,
locals greet a stranger's hand not with spear but clap-and-sway.

7.

Should one lose track of time when the strummers begin to play,
it's best to join the crowd rather than stay out of the way.

A POLE IN NEW YORK

Standing over a subway grate,
enjoying myself, I recall the phrase,
"Seasons come, seasons go,"
uttered by some king
trying on a brand new crown.
That he occupied the throne
longer than most care to know,
matters less than why
his words have stuck with me
while the steam treats me like a ghost.
The fact that I once paid
twenty bucks to tour
his walk-in closet,
where I came close to stealing
an ermine-trimmed robe,
is also beside the point, though
the uptown train's clearly running late.
Long live anyone who can
survive a barrage of honking cars
and dropped calls,
not to mention the red-eyed
storefront digits that tick-tock
across my face,
while he's trying to embody
what others have on their minds.
If, like the king, I had more time then,
I wouldn't need it now.
Warm, warmer, hot—sweat
beads on the back of my neck.
The billowing skirt says
everything I can't.

NIGHT SWIMMING

Unlike those who keep score
we've found it hard—impossible!—
to know whether it took us sixty-three
or sixty-four strokes to arrive
at the bend with a view of the other shore.
The lake was cold.
Northerly wind had stirred the wake.
From the onset I wanted to fold,
reminding my wife why
I've started going bald. With her
goggles on, she called me a big worrywart.
What I lacked in endurance,
however, I more than made up for
by holding a firm stance. Sixty-three
or sixty-four makes
no difference, unless you're stuck—
unable to touch the bottom.
Treading water in the middle,
we stared at autumn frolicking
in the trees. Orange
prevailed—if you don't count the white
jet-ski spattering like a loose atom.
Then, deep in muck, we clicked our tongues
to scare away the resident duck,
and lay side-by-side,
eager to pluck the stars and planes
zooming by. You thought you saw a buck.
But the moonlit grove was still—
the only sound I heard
was a feeble trill.

STORM

A tree in the eye of
the wind, I
trembled while clouds raced
around me.
         Then I heard
a thunder, twice,
but the bolt of lightning
I had to imagine.

LAST POEM FOR YOU

To end all suffering, more suffering
is on the way, I feel, not holding my breath.

But saying so isn't easy.
When I lose my voice like this, which happens

when I read through the night,
switching between Polish and English

and churning scraps of fiction and fact
with my tongue, I wish I had less

time to think about the future.
That man, whose hand I grabbed

in a jam-packed underpass,
calling him "dad," he said, "everything

worth remembering begins at the end."
I don't know how we made it out

alive—I only heard the muffled yelp
of someone going down.

You see, that was long ago, but still
I carry the crowd and the crowd carries me.

ELSEWHERE

Now that Poles have conquered an island
without firing a single shot—
"Ireland's beautiful," "The people kind"—
I say we follow in their footsteps

and hop on the bus, or take it to the skies,
and find this, escape that.
How long have we stood on
the bridge here, waiting for the water to pass

while it gurgles and chokes on gloves,
plastic bags, bodies, even?
Rocking, the railing resists
our climbing and spreading our arms, Love.

By the time the stars show up at five,
we'll be eating berries for supper,
making a tall fire with your flint necklace.
I'll hum your favorite tune—

something off the desert island disc—
and strike a deal with the dead below us.
If they grab or tickle us,
we'll tell them about our city's striped

smokestacks exhaling debris all day.
Or how we found the missing paperboy
in a ditch with the bike
chain around his wrists, pedaling on.

Or how it's the absence of God that makes us
behave, fall for each other,
for the guy who plays bucket drums
on the corner of Broad and First,

and for the AAA voice that says, "The tow truck
will arrive in fifteen, twenty minutes."
We always knew
we'd need help getting from B to C.

It was only yesterday that dense fog
plagued the downtown, filling
the eyes of the roaring marble lions with milk.
We had nowhere to hide.

By noon, the poor East had become
the wealthy West;
the South took on the North's way
of introducing itself with frost.

The footprints we followed
led us from one blazing oil barrel to another.
We watched people play musical chairs
with the books and lamps

they brought over to keep the fires going.
Sure enough, some kid
noticed we had brought nothing,
and they let us stay for only an hour,

though a tire, or pillows stuffed with horsehair,
would've bought us a whole day.
Our time was up before we knew it
thanks to the tower bell lashing its tongue.

I worked there one summer.
Going up and down the two hundred steps,
I lost twenty pounds.
After two weeks of pulling on the ropes

at the top of each hour, every
national holiday, tragedy or triumph,
my hands stopped bleeding.
The pay was low, but the view to die for.

On clear days the toothed mountains
shone among satellite dishes and spires.
If I looked down, I saw
tourists aiming their cameras at me.

I waved to them as one waves to ghosts
lurking in cellars, or lovers on train platforms.
And when it rained,
and water flooded my bulbous tower,

I sent signals with a flashlight to my pals,
Oscar and Maggie,
sure they were placing bets
on whose house floats away or sinks first.

I didn't want them to have fun without me.
During one heavy flood,
after the five miles between the river and us
had filled with catfish and bass,

they went out in their scuba gear
and robbed the dozen or so cars
still parked in the metered spots on our block.
They were never caught,

and I know I should've turned them in.
Instead, I quit tolling the bell
and moved closer to the airport,
where the jets unzip the sky before dawn.

Thanks to that fog, though, yesterday
was the first day I got to sleep in past nine.

Before you came, carrying
onion bagels with egg and sausage,

I dreamed of going over the state line,
beyond the strawberry field,
where I found a meadow scabbed in stones.
I enjoyed rolling them around.

But the stones quickly collected leaves
and dirt, grew too heavy
for me to push across the undulating land.
That's when a bald man appeared

out of nowhere. He said he'd take me
to bathe in nectar with voluptuous nymphs
if I moved off his property.
Instead of pockmarking it, he said,

press your ear to the ground and listen
to what the earth says.
Don't let my accent fool you, he added,
then vanished without a trace.

If you hadn't shown up, Love,
I don't know what I would've done.
Tell me, do you think I'm going crazy?
Do you think

the fog had anything to do with me
dreaming I was Sisyphus on leave?
This whole thing happened
on the fourth day of the seventh month—

but twenty-five hours later
I can't tell if the horizon resurfaced first
or the robins and the jays.
Either way, I'm glad to be back,

strolling with you across our bridge.
It was here that we first met Wanda and Hans,
the carpenter with sawdust
on his eyelids, when they bungee-jumped,

shattering the water each time.
It was here that we saw two zeppelins
fly in and drop leaflets
warning us that crime was on the rise,

while a rainbow flashed in the distance.
When we come here
it's like our first date all over again, though
now we kiss and hold hands.

But look, on the left bank Mr. Burt
is hammering a red-letter sign to his mailbox,
calling this place
something unpronounceable.

On the right bank, a fire hydrant
stuck between the locals and the newcomers
who've built their villas there,
brings them together, keeps the peace.

Nestled against two roadside shrines,
our house looks beautiful in the falling snow.
No doubt, the squirrels
dream of taking over all the floors.

Every other weekend we're back
on the roof, stomping across
the slippery slope of the autumn-brown shingles,
testing the soft spots.

Do you miss our old apartment, Love?
Once, I stood beside the chimney,

thirty feet above the ground, cleaning guano
off the siding with a squeegee.

I tried hard not to look over the edge,
down at the electric
lawnmower tangled in its cord,
the grass that to this day refuses to grow.

I found the gutters clogged
with the eerie silence
of dead flowers and headless nails
piercing the season's first film of ice.

I wanted to turn around,
climb down, unsure how one is supposed to
clean up his own mess.
Then, while I was scooping

the tea-colored water with a trowel,
panning—I saw you
at the opposite end, packing the ballast
that threatened our first home

into billowing seventeen-gallon trash bags,
as if it didn't belong to us.
But today, Love, the snow bandages
more than we can hide or ignore.

So let's follow the Poles and jump
onto the ghostly sailboat
coming our way with its engine sputtering,
like folks do in movies.

If nothing else, we'll see more
bridges, smokestacks, algae, and wrecks.
We'll be the pirates, the U.S. Navy.
We'll go skinny-dipping.

No more shifting our weight from foot to foot
to translate our need
to keep warm and move,
while our fractured shadows float in the water.

No more sticking our tongues out
and eating snowflakes, believing each one
erases a year of misery
because your fortune teller said so.

Even now, with midnight approaching
and the sky like steel
thanks to the moon dimmed
enough so as to not attract attention

to the Mexicans, Cubans or Senegalese
running or swimming for it
across borders, we must look
like hieroglyphs, exotic and maddening,

to anyone watching.
Having cancelled the cable, the mail service;
having ransacked our attic,
our Dollar-a-Day midtown storage,

we walk off the bridge, hoping
to open that door and enter the world,
and find it the same
as the last time we left it once and for all.

IN PRAISE OF TRAINS

I love riding trains. Polish trains are so slow
they take you places you wouldn't visit

otherwise. Sitting with my back to the engine,
I see everything already said and done.

PIOTR FLORCZYK was born and raised in Kraków, Poland, and moved to the United States at the age of sixteen. He is the author of *Barefoot*, a chapbook of poems, as well as *Los Angeles Sketchbook*, a volume of brief essays and photographs. He has also translated/co-translated seven collections of Polish poetry. After earning his MFA from San Diego State University in 2006, he taught at numerous colleges and universities, and now studies in the PhD in Literature and Creative Writing Program at the University of Southern California.